AURAL TEST SURVIVAL BOOK

Caroline Evans

LONDON • FRANKFURT/M • LEIPZIG • NEW YORK

Peters Edition Limited
2-6 Baches Street
London
N1 6DN
England

Tel: +44 (0)20 7553 4000
Fax: +44 (0)20 7490 4921
e-mail: sales@editionpeters.com
Internet: www.editionpeters.com

First published 2007
Revised edition published 2012

© Copyright 2007 by Hinrichsen Edition, Peters Edition Limited, London. This edition © Copyright 2012 by Hinrichsen Edition, Peters Edition Limited, London.

ISBN 978-1-84367-047-6

A catalogue record for this book is available from the British Library

All rights reserved. No part of this publication may be reproduced, stored in a retrieval system or transmitted in any form or by any means, electronic, mechanical, photocopying, recording or otherwise, without the prior written permission of the publisher.

The syllabus on which this book is based is © Copyright 2010 by The Associated Board of the Royal Schools of Music and is used by permission.

Cover design: www.adamhaystudio.com

Illustrations: Joy FitzSimmons

Printed in the UK by Halstan & Co Ltd, Amersham, Bucks.

CONTENTS

The *Aural Test Survival Book* offers a chapter-by-chapter look at responses to questions typically asked by examiners. The speed and accuracy of your responses will help you gain a better mark.

About the *Aural Test Survival Book* ..... page 4

Sing or play from memory .... page 5
. . . when the examiner says: *"I'd like you to repeat the lowest part of a three-part phrase; would you prefer to sing it or play it? . . . I'll play it twice. Here is the key-chord . . . and your starting note . . ."*

Identify the cadence .... page 10
. . . when the examiner says: *"Now tell me what cadence is at the end of this next phrase. I'll play it twice. Here is the key-chord . . ."*

Identify the chords .... page 16
. . . when the examiner says: *"Now tell me what the last three chords are. First, I'll give you the key-chord, then I'll play through the three chords you need to name. Here is the key chord . . . and the three chords . . . Now I'll stop on each chord for you to name it. Here is the key-chord again . . . First this chord . . . now this one . . . and the last . . ."*

Sing at sight .... page 23
. . . when the examiner says: *"Would you prefer to sing notes in the treble clef or bass clef? Here is a two-part phrase; I'd like you to sing the lower part while I play the upper part – number . . . on this page. First I'll give you the key-chord, your starting note and the speed; then you can have a few moments to look through and try it out loud. Here is the key-chord . . . your starting note . . . and the speed . . ."*

**Identify the modulations and
name the new keys** .... page 29
. . . when the examiner says: *"Now two modulations. Tell me where the music modulates to at the end of each passage – you will hear each of them only once. The first one begins in . . . major, and this is the key-chord . . . Where does it modulate to? . . . The second one begins in . . . minor, and this is the key-chord. Where does it modulate to?"*

Describe the music .... page 35
. . . when the examiner says: *"Listen to this piece, then describe the features that you notice. You might describe the texture, structure, character, or style and period, but mention any feature that you think is relevant."*

Find out the meaning .... page 46
. . . a list of musical terms and their meanings.

Key to Symbols

T Time

R Rhythm

I Interval

K Key

About...
...the Aural Test Survival Book

Don't be scared of aural tests! The *Aural Test Survival Book* will help you improve your listening skills and prepare you for the aural test in your music exam. You can use this book with a teacher, parent or friend, or you can practise the exercises on your own.

This book will encourage you to listen to music more actively and give you confidence to tackle the aural tests in your exam.

Try to spend a little time on aural skills as part of your regular practice. You already have your examination pieces, studies and scales. Now here's your own book of aural skills!

Caroline Evans

A note to teachers

The material in the *Aural Test Survival Book* corresponds to the Associated Board's aural requirements for music examinations and is suitable for all instrumentalists. Many of the tests are common to other examination boards and so students preparing for any music exam will find the book useful.

You can try out the activities in your lessons, or you can set them for your students to complete at home. The format of the book encourages students to think in terms of four important elements of music: Time, Rhythm, Interval and Key.

SING OR PLAY FROM MEMORY

Test 8A(i)

When the examiner says:

"I'd like you to repeat the lowest part of a three-part phrase; would you prefer to sing it or play it? . . . I'll play it twice. Here is the key-chord . . . and your starting note . . ."

What should you do?

Decide with your teacher long before the exam whether you are going to sing or play this test.

Sing the notes of the key-chord in your head, noting whether it is major or minor.

Listen carefully to the *lowest* part, focusing on the first part of the phrase in the first playing, and on the second part of the phrase in the second playing.

Concentrate on both the rhythm and pitch.

Sing or play the lowest part of what has just been played on the piano. You may play your response on the piano or on your own instrument.

What you need to know

The examiner will ask whether you wish to sing or play this test.

A three-part phrase in a major or minor key (with up to three sharps or flats) will be played twice on the piano. The lowest part will have a range of up to an octave. You should sing or play the lowest part only (at a different octave, if necessary).

Test 8A(i)

The examiner will start by playing the key--chord and starting note. A count-in of two bars (for example: 1-2-3-1-2-3) will be given.

When you sing or play back the lowest part, there will be no piano accompaniment.

If you are playing a transposing instrument (for example, clarinet or trumpet), you will be told your playing key and starting note so that it will sound at the same pitch as the piano.

Work out the key signature for the named key before you start playing.

If necessary, the examiner will play the phrase again and allow you a second attempt, although this will affect your mark.

How should you do it?

Before the music starts:
- Hum or play quietly your starting note.

While listening:
- As soon as the examiner gives the count-in, tap your toe gently in time right through to the end of the test.
- Focus on the lowest part of the phrase and follow its shape in your head.
- Listen carefully to the rhythm of the lowest part as well as the note pitches – the rhythm is just as important. Tap the rhythm with your hand against your side.
- Listen to the key-chord and starting note and keep them in mind throughout the test.

When you start singing or playing:
- Keep tapping your toe gently in time while singing or playing the lowest part.

Test 8A(i)

- Don't pause after the examiner has finished playing the second time – come straight in and keep to the same speed as the examiner, particularly when the phrase ends on a long note.
- Sing "lah" to each note. If you prefer, you may hum or whistle, although it is hard to whistle accurately.
- Imitate the articulation and dynamics.
- Don't cut short any notes that are long.

At all times:

- **Stand tall**
- **Sound confident**
- **Sing/play out**

Training session

Play some major and minor scales and arpeggios (with key signatures of up to three sharps or flats) on your own instrument (if voice is your instrument, then sing). Play at a comfortable speed and tap your toe gently to keep in time.

After you have played each scale or arpeggio, sing it. In order for it to be comfortable for your voice, you may need to sing it an octave higher or lower than you played it.

Keep to the speed you played before, and still tap your toe gently to keep in time. Sing "lah" or "doh" to each note, and make sure each note is separated. As you sing, try to see the shape of the music in your head.

Play then sing the scale of E minor, then look at the following music. Notice the fall–rise–fall shape of the lowest part, and the repeat of the rhythm of the first bar in the third bar.

Test 8A(i)

J. S. Bach

First, tap the rhythm of the lowest part on your side. If you can play the keyboard, play all three parts (if not, ask someone who can). Then sing the lowest part.

Now look away from the music and try to play or sing the lowest part from memory. It may help if you visualise the fingering you would use.

You will find that you have to concentrate harder when other parts are played at the same time. So begin by dividing the melody in the lowest part into two sections.

Play then sing a C major scale and arpeggio, then look at the following music. Notice the arpeggiated patterns in the lowest part.

J. Haydn (adapted)

Tap the rhythm of the lowest part on your side, then play it, then sing. Start by dividing it into two sections.

How to improve further

Listen to some music you don't know and sing or play back short phrases of the lowest part. Use the radio or TV and press the mute button while you sing or play.

The aim of the test

The purpose of this test is to train your ear to follow the lowest part, and to expand your musical memory.

SURVIVAL TIPS Test 8A(i)

1. Don't worry about the sound of your own voice – concentrate on singing in tune and in time.

2. Close your eyes to help you concentrate. Try to "block out" what the upper parts are playing.

3. Concentrate on the first half of the phrase in the first playing, the second half in the second playing.

4. Take a deep breath before you begin to sing – and again after the first half of the phrase if necessary – so that you don't run out of air before the end.

5. Use bright vowels – "lah" is usually best – and don't slide up or down to notes.

6. Sing or play something, even if you're unsure – just get the rhythm right and end on the tonic. Ask for a second attempt if you think you can do better, but this will affect your mark.

Follow the TRaK:

T Time: tap your toe in time with the beat while listening, singing or playing.

R Rhythm: listen carefully to the rhythm as well as the note pitches and don't cut long notes short.

K Key: listen carefully to the key-chord and starting note so that you sing in tune. If you play the test, work out the key signature first.

IDENTIFY THE CADENCE

Test 8A(ii)

When the examiner says:

"Now tell me what cadence is at the end of this next phrase. I'll play it twice. Here is the key-chord . . ."

What should you do?

Identify the cadence at the end of the phrase as perfect, imperfect, interrupted or plagal.

What you need to know

A cadence is a resting point or breathing place in music – similar to punctuation in a sentence.

There are several types of cadence, depending on which chords are used. For this test, you will be asked whether a cadence is perfect, imperfect, interrupted or plagal. Here are the chords used in these cadences:

Perfect   Dominant (in root position or in first or second inversion) or dominant seventh to tonic

Imperfect   Tonic (root position, first or second inversion), supertonic (root position or first inversion), or subdominant to dominant

Interrupted   Dominant or dominant seventh to submediant

Plagal   Subdominant to tonic

The phrase will be a continuation of that played in part 8A(i). It will be in four-part harmony in either a major or a minor key.

The examiner will always begin by playing the key-chord and will play the phrase twice.

Test 8A(ii)

How should you do it?

While listening:

- Listen to the key-chord. Keep the tonic in your head until the end of the phrase.
- Listen to the movement of the chords at the end of the phrase.
- Ask your yourself if the phrase has returned to the key-chord via the dominant chord (perfect cadence) or subdominant (plagal cadence), or whether it sounds as if it is "halfway" (imperfect cadence), or a "false close" (interrupted cadence).
- Concentrate on the bass (lowest) notes.

When you answer:

- Before you respond, double-check by humming the last two bass notes and the tonic note.
- State whether the cadence is perfect, imperfect, interrupted or plagal.

Training session

Perfect cadence

A perfect cadence, or "full close", leads firmly back to the home key and has a feeling of completion. It is made up of the dominant or dominant seventh chord, followed by the tonic chord.

Here are perfect cadences in the keys of C major and E minor. The chords are named with roman numerals. The seventh in the dominant chords is added in brackets. Play the key-chord, and then play or sing the notes as spread chords.

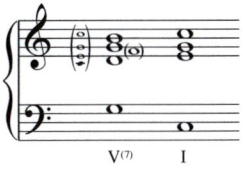
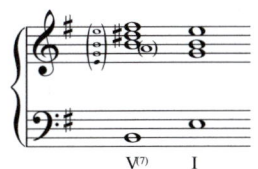

Test 8A(ii)

Imperfect cadence

An imperfect cadence, or a "half close", sounds as if the music should lead on to another phrase. An imperfect cadence always finishes on the dominant chord. In the exam, it will normally be preceded by the tonic (either in root position, or in first or second inversion), the supertonic (in root position or first inversion) or the subdominant chord (in root position).

Here are imperfect cadences in the keys of B flat major, G major and A minor. In the first, the dominant chord is preceded by the tonic, in the second it is preceded by the first inversion of the supertonic, and in the third it is preceded by the subdominant. The chords are named with roman numerals. Play the key-chord, and then play or sing the notes as spread chords. Note that if the second inversion of the tonic is used, the bass stays on the same note.

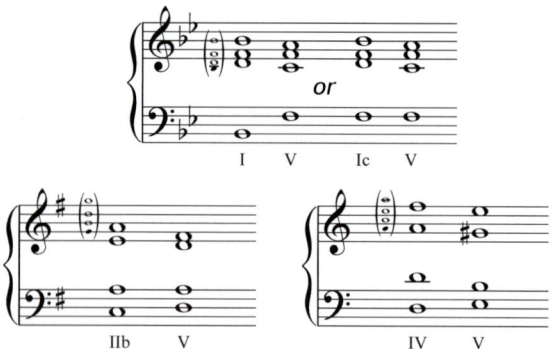

Interrupted cadence

An interrupted cadence, or a "false close", sounds as if the flow of the music has been interrupted and leaves the listener in suspense. It surprises the listener: the dominant goes not down to the tonic to form a perfect cadence, but up to the submediant.

Here are interrupted cadences in the keys of A major and G minor. Play the key-chord, and then play or sing the notes as spread chords. Note the ascending step

Test 8A(ii)

in the bass from the dominant to the submediant. Take care not to confuse this with the ascending step from subdominant to dominant in an imperfect cadence.

Note that in a major key the submediant chord is minor, and in a minor key the submediant chord is major.

Plagal cadence

A plagal cadence is often called the "Amen" cadence, because it is the cadence used in churches to sing amen. In a plagal cadence, the tonic chord is preceded by a subdominant chord. A plagal cadence does not have such a strong pull to the tonic as in a perfect cadence because the subdominant chord does not contain the leading note.

Here are plagal cadences in the keys of G major and D minor. Play the key-chord, and then play or sing the notes as spread chords.

Here are some extracts of music similar to what you will hear in your exam. Which extract finishes with a perfect cadence, which with an imperfect cadence, which with an interrupted cadence and which with a plagal cadence? Remember that a perfect cadence finishes on the key-chord and sounds "finished", a plagal cadence also ends on the key-chord but sounds less conclusive, an imperfect cadence finishes on the dominant chord and sounds as if it

Test 8A(ii)

should continue with another phrase, while an interrupted cadence sounds as if the music is left hanging.

How to improve further

Look at the piano part of the first sixteen bars of a piece you are learning. Work out where the cadences are and see which of them are perfect, imperfect, interrupted or plagal cadences.

Listen to any music on the radio or TV and identify the cadence points.

The aim of the test

The purpose of this test is to encourage you to hear the effect that different cadences have in shaping a phrase.

SURVIVAL TIPS   Test 8A(ii)

1. Keep the tonic note in your head throughout the test.

2. Listen for a feeling of "strong completion" (perfect cadence), of "leading on" (imperfect cadence), of "unexpected interruption" (interrupted cadence), or "amen completion" (plagal cadence).

3. Before answering, double-check your answer by humming the last bass note and the tonic note – if they are the same it is either a perfect or a plagal cadence, if they are a fifth apart it is an imperfect cadence, if they are a sixth apart it is an interrupted cadence.

4. Answer straight away.

Home, halfway, hanging or amen?

K Key: listen carefully to the key-chord and keep the tonic in your head throughout the test. Decide if the cadence is "strongly home" (perfect), "halfway" (imperfect), "hanging" (interrupted) or "amen" (plagal).

IDENTIFY THE CHORDS — Test 8A(iii)

When the examiner says:

"Now tell me what the last three chords are. First, I'll give you the key-chord, then I'll play through the three chords you need to name. Here is the key chord . . . and the three chords . . . Now I'll stop on each chord for you to name it. Here is the key-chord again . . . First this chord . . . now this one . . . and the last . . ."

What should you do?

Listen carefully as the examiner names and plays the key-chord followed by the last three chords, forming the cadential progression you have just heard in the previous part of the test (8A(ii) on page 10).

The chords you have to identify will then be played again, each followed by a brief pause. Name the chords during the pauses.

Concentrate on the bass (lowest) notes.

Remember that you already know the last two chords, having identified the cadence for the previous part of the test.

What you need to know

The key-chord will be named and played again.

The chords will be in four-part harmony.

You can name the chords using their technical names (for example, first inversion of the tonic), roman numerals (for example, Ib), or key names (for example, G major in first inversion). The chords will be three of the following possibilities:

Test 8A(iii)

Tonic: root position, first inversion or second inversion (I, Ib or Ic)
Supertonic: root position or first inversion (I or Ib)
Subdominant: root position (IV)
Dominant: root position, first inversion or second inversion (V, Vb or Vc)
Dominant seventh: root position (V^7)
Submediant: root position (VI)

How should you do it?

While listening:

- Remember which chords make the cadence you named in the previous part of the test (8A(ii) on page 10).
- Listen to the key-chord, singing the notes in your head.
- If necessary, adjust your answer to the previous part of the test if you realise you identified the cadence incorrectly.
- Concentrate on the bass (lowest) notes.

When you answer:

- Before you respond, double-check by humming the bass note of each chord and the tonic note.

Describe the chords using their technical names (for example, dominant in second inversion), roman numerals (for example, Vc) or key names (for example, D major in second inversion).

Training session

In addition to stating whether each chord is tonic, dominant, subdominant, supertonic or submediant, you have to decide whether it is in root position, first inversion or second inversion. It is always the lowest note in the chord which tells you this – which is why it is important to concentrate on the bass notes in this test.

Test 8A(iii)

Tonic chord in first and second inversion

Sing or play as spread chords the root position, first inversion and second inversion chords of G major:

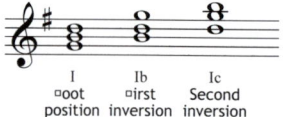

Here are three common chord progressions in G major using the tonic chord in inversion. Play the key-chord first, then play the notes of each chord. Note how the bass part moves in each of these progressions.

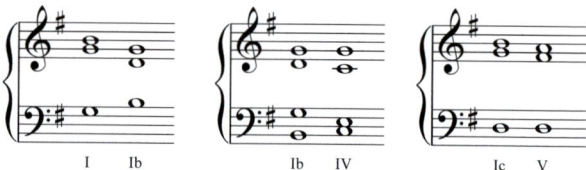

Supertonic chord in first inversion

Sing or play as spread chords the root position and first inversion supertonic chords in the key of B flat major. Play the key-chord first:

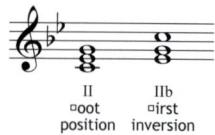

Here are three common chord progressions in B flat major using the supertonic chord. Play the key-chord as a spread chord first, then the notes of each chord. Once again, note how the bass part moves in each progression.

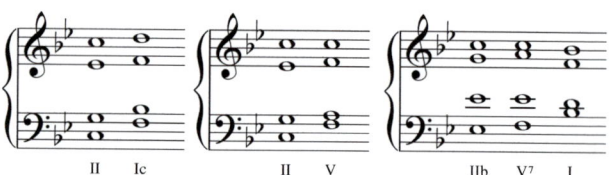

Test 8A(iii)

Dominant chords in first and second inversion, and dominant seventh

Play or sing the key-chord of D minor as a spread chord. Then sing or play the dominant chord in root position, first inversion and second inversion. Finally, play the dominant seventh.

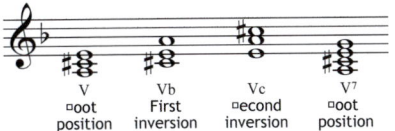

Note that the dominant chord in a minor key is a major chord.

Play or sing the key-chord of D minor again, then play the following chords as spread chords. Note how the bass part moves, and that adding the seventh to the dominant gives a stronger pull towards the tonic.

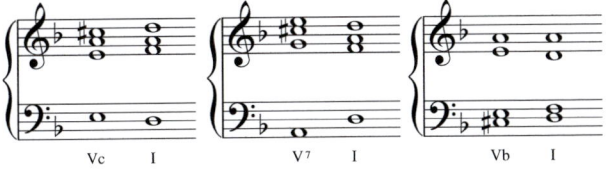

Here are some common chord progressions in four-part harmony, similar to those you would hear in your exam. The chords are named with roman numerals.

First, look at how the chords, particularly the bass notes, move towards the cadence. Play the bass line, and then play the complete chords as broken chords. Play them several times, familiarising yourself with their sound.

Perfect cadence

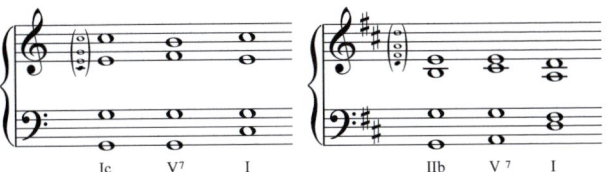

Test 8A(iii)

Imperfect cadence

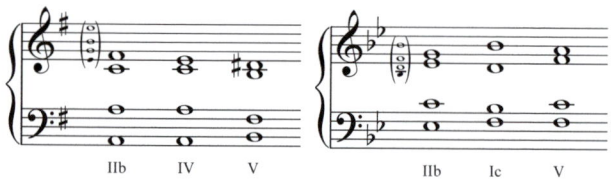

Interrupted cadence

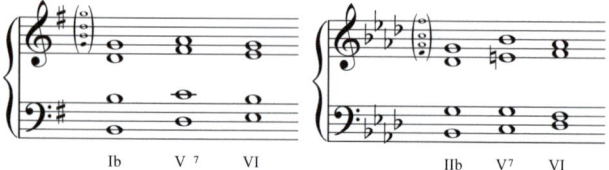

Plagal cadence

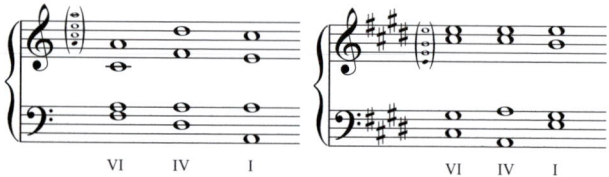

Ask someone to play these chord progressions for you and see if you can identify which one is which.

Here are three examples of the whole of test 8A. Each part of the test is indicated on these examples. Remember that the examiner will play the relevant part of the music again for each section of the test.

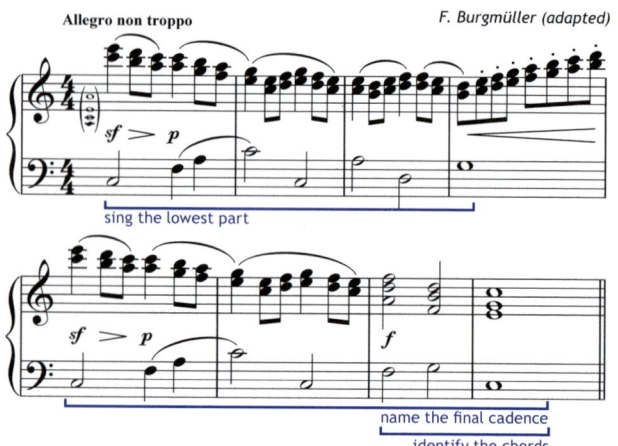

Test 8A(iii)

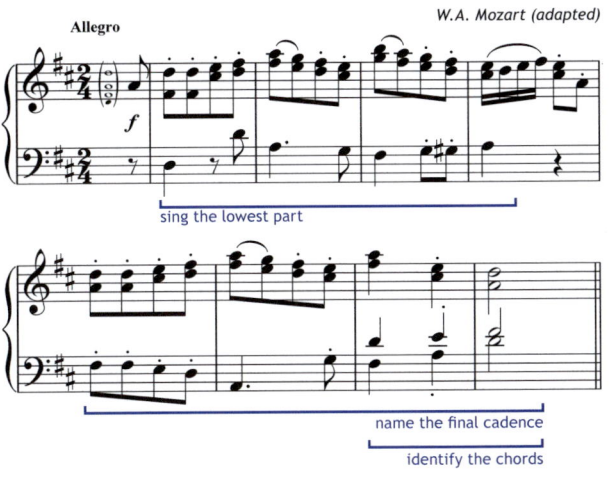

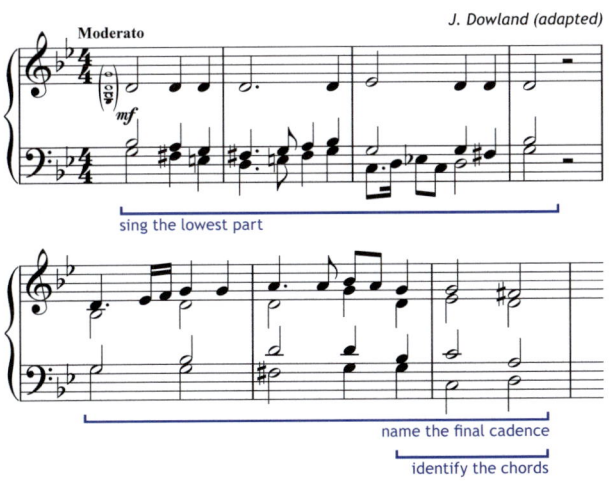

How to improve further

When you have identified the cadence points in the first sixteen bars of a piece you are learning (you did this on page 14 of this book), name the three chords forming the cadential progression and write the roman numerals underneath. Remember to write whether the chords are in root position, first inversion or second inversion, and whether they are ordinary dominant chords or dominant sevenths.

The aim of the test

The purpose of this test is to understand the relationship between chords.

SURVIVAL TIPS Test 8A(iii)

1. Make sure that the chords you name in this test correspond to the cadence you named in test 8A(ii). If, when you do this test, you think you stated the wrong cadence in the previous test, correct yourself now.

2. Double-check by humming the bass notes and the tonic note, and work out the intervals between them.

3. Dominant seventh (V^7) chords sound very rich and full, and create a stronger pull towards the tonic than a dominant chord on its own.

4. If you are not sure whether the chords are in root position, first inversion or second inversion, or whether the dominant is a dominant seventh, make an intelligent guess. You may get it right, but if you give no answer you will get nothing right.

   tonic
   supertonic
   subdominant
   dominant
   dominant seventh
   submediant

Figure the bass

K Listen to the key-chord. Keep the tonic note in your head and relate it to the bass notes.

SING AT SIGHT
Test 8B

When the examiner says:

"Would you prefer to sing notes in the treble clef or bass clef? Here is a two-part phrase; I'd like you to sing the lower part while I play the upper part – number . . . on this page. First I'll give you the key-chord, your starting note and the speed; then you can have a few moments to look through and try it out loud. Here is the key-chord . . . your starting note . . . and the speed . . ."

What should you do?

Decide with your teacher before the exam whether you will sing this test from the treble or bass clef. Tell the examiner on the day.

Look carefully at the notes in the score. Sing the lower part only. Begin when the examiner has counted you in.

What you need to know

You will be given a score which contains several examples of this test. You will be told which one to sing.

The test will consist of a short phrase in two parts. You will be asked to sing the lower part while the examiner plays the upper part on the piano.

The music will be in a major or minor key with up to four sharps or flats. Your starting note and finishing note will not necessarily be the tonic.

Your part will be within the range of an octave.

Test 8B

The examiner will name and play the key-chord and starting note and give the speed.

You will be given about 15 seconds to look through the test. Before you start singing, the key-chord and starting note will be repeated, and a count-in of two bars given.

You may ask for a second attempt if necessary, but this will affect your mark.

How should you do it?

While preparing:

- Listen to the key-chord. Sing the notes in your head as soon as the key-chord is sounded. Your starting note will be the first, third or fifth note of the chord - hum it quietly.

- Look to see if any notes in the score are in the key-chord that you have just heard.

- Pick up the beat as soon as it is indicated by gently tapping your toe.

- Note the time signature and tap the rhythm on your side while you look at the note pitches.

- Look at the key signature. Check to see if it affects any notes in the test.

- Sing quietly to yourself as you work out interval steps or leaps. Do this by humming up or down from the preceding note, or from the tonic. It may help to use the opening interval of a well-known melody (see page 25).

When you start singing:

- Continue to tap your toe gently in time with the beat.

Test 8B

- Sing "lah" to each note. If you prefer, you may hum or whistle, although it is difficult to whistle accurately.
- Keep the starting note in your head and be aware of the key throughout the piece.
- If you are not sure about a pitch, sing something but get the rhythm right.
- Observe the articulation and dynamics.

Training session

Most phrases are based on the scale of the given key and its primary chords (the chords of the tonic, dominant and subdominant). So a melody in G minor will often be made up of phrases using the following patterns:

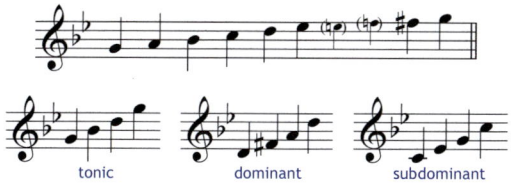

Work out the intervals between the notes of the scale and chords.

Play and sing some other major and minor scales and their primary triads (with key signatures of up to four sharps or flats). Choose a comfortable tempo.

Associating an interval with a well-known tune makes it easier to sing without having to count the interval. Here are the opening phrases of some well-known tunes with the intervals indicated.

All through the night:

Sleep my child and peace at-tend thee, All through the night.

Test 8B

Frère Jacques:

Daisy, Daisy:

Swing low:

Here comes the bride (Wagner's *Bridal March*):

Twinkle, twinkle little star:

The Entertainer:

My bonnie lies over the ocean:

Play these phrases on your instrument and sing them back like an echo. Play the notes of the key-chord first. Once you have sung the whole phrase, sing just the two notes that make the interval. Then sing the two notes in reverse order.

You may sometimes see an interval of an octave. This is quite easy to pitch: think of the first two notes of *Somewhere over the rainbow*, or *I'm singin' in the rain*. For more obscure intervals, go "via" an easier interval. So, for example, sing an augmented fifth by hearing a perfect fifth in your head before singing a semitone higher. Always check to see whether the interval might be easier than you think - a diminished fourth, for example, is the same as a major third.

Always try to hear the notes in your head before you sing.

Here is a short two-bar phrase, similar to what you will see in the exam. Play then hum the key-chord and starting note first. Then sing the note pitches of the lower part – don't worry about the rhythm to start with. The larger intervals are marked – use the well-known tunes to work out these intervals. Note that the phrase is a combination of the tonic scale and the tonic chord.

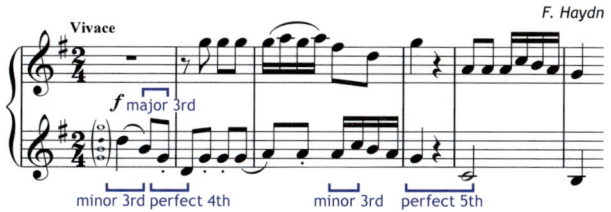

Now tap the rhythm on your side. Look to see how the rhythm of the lower part fits with the upper part, and whether there are any passages where the rhythm is the same in both parts.

Finally, sing the lower part with the correct rhythm. Ask someone to play the upper part while you sing.

Here is another example for you to try. Play the key-chord and starting note first. Look out for the semitones and remember to work out any intervals larger than a second. Check how the rhythm of the lower part fits with that of the upper part.

Test 8B

J. S. Bach (adapted)

How to improve further

Look at any piece of music you are learning (or its piano accompaniment) and try to sight-sing the lower part in the first four bars of any line. First concentrate on pitching the notes accurately. Then sing with the correct rhythm. Try sight-singing the first bar of another line.

The aim of the test

This test develops your "inner ear", which helps you to hear the sound in your head before singing or playing.

SURVIVAL TIPS

Test 8B

1. Look ahead to each interval before you sing it and keep counting. Don't guess.
2. Use bright vowels – "lah" is usually best (not "ler").
3. Don't forget that the upper part can help you.
4. Take a deep breath before you start, and another after the first part of the phrase if necessary.
5. Don't sing crotchets when you see quavers, and observe any rests.
6. Try to hear the notes in your head before you sing.
7. Don't panic – sing something. Try at least to get the rhythm correct. Ask for a second attempt if necessary, although this will affect your mark.

Learn the TRIK:

T Time: look at the time signature and keep counting in your head.

R Rhythm: the rhythm is just as important as the note pitches.

I Interval: work out the interval steps and leaps.

K Key: listen carefully to the key-chord and starting note. Sing the notes in your head as soon as the chord is played. Look carefully at the key signature.

IDENTIFY THE MODULATIONS Test 8C

When the examiner says:

"Now two modulations. Tell me where the music modulates to at the end of each passage – you will hear each of them only once. The first one begins in . . . major, and this is the key-chord . . . Where does it modulate to? . . . The second one begins in . . . minor, and this is the key-chord. Where does it modulate to?"

What should you do?

State whether the music has modulated to the dominant, subdominant, relative minor or relative major, or state what the new key is.

The examiner will then repeat the test with a different passage of music.

What you need to know

The first passage will start in a major key and the second will start in a minor key. The key-chord will be played and named.

The modulations will be to the dominant, subdominant, relative minor (from a major key) or relative major (from a minor key).

Passages that start in a minor key may modulate to either the dominant major or dominant minor, but you only need to specify "dominant" in such cases.

Each passage will be played only once.

How should you do it?

While listening:

- Listen to the key-chord, keeping the tonic in your head throughout the test.

Test 8C

- Remember the name of the key given by the examiner.
- Listen for a sharpened fourth, indicating a modulation to the dominant, a flattened seventh, indicating a modulation to the subdominant, or a move from major to minor, or from minor to major.
- Concentrate particularly on the bass notes at the end of the passage.

When you answer:

- Double-check your answer by working out the interval between the last bass note and the tonic note.
- Identify the modulation as dominant, subdominant, relative minor or relative major, or name the new key (for example, G major).

Training session

A modulation is a change of key. In this test, it will be marked by a perfect cadence in the new key.

Play the following melody, which starts in E major and modulates to the dominant (B major). Notice how the sharpened fourth (A sharp) becomes the leading note in the new key and pulls the melody towards the dominant. When you have played it in E major, play it in some other keys.

Here is a passage of music similar to what you will hear in the exam. Once again, the sharpened fourth pulls the music towards the dominant.

D. Scarlatti (adapted)

Test 8C

Now play the following melody, which starts in F major and modulates to the subdominant (B flat major). Notice how the flattened seventh (E flat) pulls the melody towards the subdominant. Note also that the third note of the scale (A) becomes the leading note in the new key. When you have played the melody in F major, play it in some other keys.

Here is a passage of music similar to what you will hear in the exam. Once again, the flattened seventh and the third of the scale pull the music towards the subdominant.

G. F. Handel (adapted)

Play the following melody, which starts in B flat major and modulates to the relative minor (G minor). Listen for the F sharp, which becomes the leading note in the new key, and for the minor tonality in the last two bars. When you have played it in B flat major, play it in some other keys.

Here is a passage of music similar to what you will hear in the exam, which modulates to the relative minor.

Test 8C

C. Gluck (adapted)

Play the following melody, which starts in F minor and modulates to the relative major (A flat major). Listen for the G, which becomes the leading note in the new key, and for the major tonality in the last two bars. When you have played it in F minor, play it in some other keys.

Here is a passage of music which modulates to the relative major.

J. Haydn (adapted)

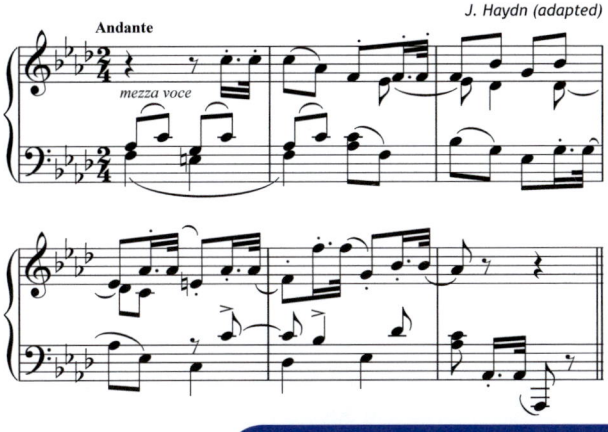

How to improve further

Identify modulations to the dominant, subdominant and relative major/minor in some pieces you are learning. Identify where the sharpened fourth, flattened seventh and leading notes first appear.

The aim of the test

The purpose of this test is to develop your perception of the tonal structure of music.

SURVIVAL TIPS

Test 8C

1. "Look sharp" – if you hear a note sharpened, then it probably indicates a modulation to the dominant.

2. "Fall flat" – if you hear a note flattened, the modulation is probably to the subdominant.

3. The leading note of the new key will precede the tonic of the new key, in either the upper or one of the inner parts.

4. Double-check your answer by working out the interval between the last bass note and the tonic note.

   dominant
   subdominant
   relative minor
   relative major

5. If you prefer, you can name the new key, but make sure you name a key that is the dominant, subdominant, relative minor or relative major of the starting key.

Key move

K Listen to the key-chord. Keep the tonic note in your head and relate it to the bass note of the last chord.

DESCRIBE THE MUSIC — Test 8D

When the examiner says:

"Listen to this piece, then describe the features that you notice. You might describe the texture, structure, character, or style and period, but mention any feature that you think is relevant."

What should you do?

The examiner will play a piece of music and then ask you to describe it. Mention most or all of the features below.

Dynamics
   (loud/quiet, gradually getting louder/quieter)

Articulation
   (detached, smooth, accented or ornamented)

Tempo
   (speed)

Time
   (number of beats in a bar; metre)

Tonality
   (major, minor, modal or atonal)

Rhythm
   (the pattern of note values)

Character
   (distinctive features)

Style and period
   (what the music sounds like; when it was composed)

Texture
   (think in terms of thick or thin)

Structure (including phrase structure)
   (how the piece is constructed; regular or irregular phrases)

Test 8D

What you need to know

Learn the meanings of the following terms and Italian words. Try to use them in your answer where appropriate.

Dynamics

fairly loud; loud; very loud
mezzo forte; *forte*; *fortissimo*
symbols: *mf*; *f*; *ff*

fairly quiet; quiet; very quiet
mezzo piano; *piano*; *pianissimo*
symbols: *mp*; *p*; *pp*

gradually getting louder
crescendo
symbol: ──═══ (an "opening hairpin")

gradually getting quieter
diminuendo
symbol: ═══── (a "closing hairpin")

Articulation

detached
staccato; *semi-staccato*
symbols: ♩ ♩; ♩♩ ♩♩

smooth
legato
symbol: ⌒ (a slur)

ornamented notes
trill; mordent; turn; acciaccatura; appoggiatura
symbols: *tr*; ∿; ∞; ♪; ♪

accented notes
sforzando; *tenuto*
symbols: *sfz*, *sf*; ─ ♩

Tempo

performance instructions
adagio; *moderato*; *allegro*; *presto*

gradually getting faster
accelerando (*accel.*); *stringendo* (*string.*)

gradually getting slower
rallentando (*rall.*) or *ritardando* (*ritard.*)

in flexible time
tempo rubato

Time, metre
number of beats in a bar (2, 3 or 4); simple or compound

Tonality
major, minor, modal, atonal, chromatic, dissonant, jazz chords

Rhythm
regular or irregular; describe rhythmic figures (e.g. dotted rhythm, triplets, syncopation), swung rhythms

Character
distinctive features; use descriptions like: sombre, minor key with chromaticism, simple melody with decoration, static harmony, gentle

Style and period
Style is the manner of writing, or what the music sounds like. Use words like: balanced phrases with regular cadence points; moderate pitch range; variety of textures.

Here are the main musical periods, with approximate dates:

Baroque: 1600–1750

Classical: 1750–1790

Romantic: 1790–1910

Early 20th century: 1910–1940

Contemporary: 1940–now

Texture
homophonic: chordal, melody usually in the upper part with chords or broken chords in the lower part

contrapuntal: two or more melodic lines of equal importance combined together

Structure (including phrase structure)
You may hear a clear structure to the piece. For example:

Test 8D

a first section (A) followed by a second section (B) with different material – this is known as binary form

a first section (A) followed by a second section (B), which is then followed by a repeat of the first section (A) – this is known as ternary form

an introduction (often consisting of just a few chords) followed by a main theme

phrase structure – regular (often 4-bar) phrase structure, or irregular (for instance, 5-bar followed by 3-bar)

Although you should know about other larger-scale forms – theme and variations, rondo and sonata – they are unlikely to be used in the exam.

You will only need to mention two-thirds of the features above in order to receive full marks.

How should you do it?

Before the music starts:
- Be prepared to describe all aspects of the music.

While listening:
Try to listen for some or all of the following features: dynamics, articulation, tempo, time, tonality, rhythm, character, style and period, texture and structure. It is difficult to remember them all but at least be prepared to describe: character, texture, and style and period.

When you answer:
- Try to use Italian words like *sforzando*, *dolce*, *rubato* and *ritenuto* in your answers.
- If you are describing the character of the piece, think about its distinctive features and mood.
- If you are describing the style of the piece, think of the period in which it might have been composed.

Test 8D

- Be ready to describe the music fully rather than give one-word answers. Respond straight away. If necessary, the examiner will prompt you with questions about a particular feature.

Training session

You will not be expected to be an expert in the history of music – but be prepared to suggest a possible composer or to indicate in which period you think the music was composed. It's a good idea to relate what you hear to what you know: ask yourself if it sounds similar to music you have played, sung or heard.

Here are some typical features of musical styles to listen for. They will help you work out when a piece was composed.

BAROQUE (c.1600–c.1750)

Dynamics: restrained

Articulation: ornaments (turns, mordents, etc.), often semi-staccato

Tempo: remains constant

Rhythm: regular, often dotted

Character: elegant, well-defined phrases

Style: dance forms like gavotte, minuet, allemande, courante, sarabande, gigue

Texture: often contrapuntal

Structure: often binary (AB)

Limited compass of the piano; no pedalling

Composers: J.S. Bach, Handel, Vivaldi, Purcell, Rameau, D. Scarlatti, Couperin, Corelli

CLASSICAL period (c.1750–c.1790)

Dynamics: more contrasted than in baroque music

Articulation: accented notes (e.g. sforzando); some ornaments

Tonality: major and minor

Rhythm: regular, often flowing

Test 8D

Character: balanced phrases, flowing melodies
Texture: often homophonic
Structure: clearly-defined forms; sonata forms; balanced phrase structure
Some pedalling

    Composers: Haydn, Mozart, Beethoven, Dussek, Salieri, Clementi

ROMANTIC period (c.1790–c.1910)

Dynamics: contrasted; extensive use of *cresc.* and *dim.*
Articulation: flamboyant flourishes
Tempo: *rubato* is common
Tonality: chromaticism; modulations to unexpected keys
Rhythm: irregular groupings
Character: rich harmonic writing, decorated melodies
Style: dance forms (like waltzes, mazurkas and polonaises); descriptive music (describing things like streams, pictures, reflections and mythical characters)
Texture: normally homophonic
Considerable use of the pedal; wider range of the piano used

 Composers: Schubert, Chopin, Schumann, Tchaikovsky, Fauré, Wagner, Brahms, Grieg, Mendelssohn

EARLY 20TH CENTURY (c.1910–c.1940)

Dynamics: wide dynamic range
Articulation: clearly defined and specific
Time: frequent changes of time signature
Tonality: dissonance and chord clusters; atonal (no fixed key); serialism; large intervals and disjointed melody; modal
Rhythm: changes of metre; syncopation
Character: dramatic; dissonant harmonies; complex rhythms; syncopation
Style: impressionism; jazz; folk; extremities of instrument used

 Composers: Debussy, Ravel, Vaughan Williams, Gershwin, Stravinsky, Prokofiev, Shostakovich, Bartók

Test 8D

CONTEMPORARY (c.1940–now)
Dynamics: varied and contrasted
Articulation: varied
Tonality: major and minor; modal
Rhythm: repetition of short rhythms
Character: cross rhythms
Style: lyrical, influenced by other styles, minimalism (world music, jazz, rock)

Composers: Steve Reich, John Tavener, Philip Glass, Michael Nyman, Harrison Birtwistle, Pierre Boulez, Richard Rodney Bennett, Peter Maxwell Davies

Listen to some music on the TV, radio or on a CD. Decide whether the music you are listening to is:

- fairly loud (*mezzo forte*), loud (*forte*) or very loud (*fortissimo)*, or fairly quiet (*mezzo piano*), quiet (*piano*) or very quiet (*pianissimo*)
- getting gradually louder (*crescendo*) or gradually quieter (*diminuendo)*
- detached (*staccato*), smooth (*legato*), accented or ornamented
- playful (*scherzando*), slow (adagio) or moderate (moderato); getting gradually faster (acc*elerando)* or gradually slower (*rallentando*)
- in a major or minor key

Can you also describe the character or mood? Be aware of any characteristic rhythms that might feature. Look at pages 46–48 for some useful words.

Lastly, how would you describe the style of the music? What about its structure, texture and rhythm?

The examiner might ask you specific questions. Here are some examples of what you might be asked, with the sort of answers you could give:

Test 8D

Dynamics

Question: "What can you say about the dynamics?"
Answer: "Overall they were quiet – between *pianissimo* and *mezzo piano*, but there seemed to be a different dynamic and colour for every note."

Articulation

Question: "Can you describe the varied articulation in this piece?"
Answer: "The upper part was mostly *legato* and the lower part lightly *staccato*. But there was a passage in the middle when both parts were very *staccato* and *marcato*. And there were a couple of *legato* flourishes."

Tempo

Question: "What tempo marking would be appropriate for this piece?"
Answer: "As it's rather stately and processional, possibly *largo* or *adagio*."

Time

Question: "What time was this piece in?"
Answer: "It was in 4-time."

Tonality

Question: "What can you say about the use of harmony and tonality?"
Answer: "The piece began in a minor key and modulated to a major key – I think to the relative major."

Rhythm

Question: "Was it played in strict time?"
Answer: "No, there was some *rubato*."
Question: "What can you say about the rhythm?"
Answer: "The tied notes give a slightly syncopated effect."

Character

Question: "What in the music gave the

piece its character?"
Answer: "There were thick textures and a cantabile melody"

Question: "What can you say about the character?"
Answer: "It had a light-hearted mood with swinging rhythms"

Style and period

Question: "When do you think this was written?"
Answer: "Probably early 20th century."
Question: ". . . and what makes you think that?"
Answer: ". . . because, although it was tonal, there were some unusual harmonies and dissonance."
Question: "What can you say about the character of this piece?"
Answer: "It was *piano* and light – *leggiero*, with the pedal creating drifts of sound in the lower part."

Texture

Question: "What can you say about the use of texture in this piece?"
Answer: "It was chordal and harmonic, with the melody in the upper part. The chords in the upper part were in thirds."

Structure and form

Question: "What can you say about the structure of this piece?"
Answer: "It was ternary form – ABA"
Question: ". . . and how did the character of the B section differ from the A section?"
Answer: "The A section was chordal whereas the B section was lighter, scalic, and swirled up and down."
Question: "What is the purpose of the first two bars?"
Answer: "They form an introduction, perhaps inviting people to take their position for the dance."

Test 8D

The examiner will not normally lead the discussion with a question but ask you to describe what you heard.

This is an example of what you might say: "The piece was mostly *mezzo forte* with a legato upper part and a lightly detached lower part. The tempo remained constant throughout and it was in two time. It had a lively, dance-like character with a contrapuntal texture. It was in binary form and was composed in the Baroque period - perhaps by Bach."

Here is another example: "There was a four-bar introduction followed by two main sections – the second section had the same tune as the first, but an octave higher. It was *forte* and had an upbeat tempo. It was in a minor key and the swung rhythms made it sound quite cool. It was probably composed recently."

How to improve further

See if you can describe the pieces you are learning at the moment as fully as possible. Then do the same with music you hear on the TV or radio.

Try listening to the following and see if you can identify some of the typical features from each period:

BAROQUE: Rameau, *Les Indes Galantes*
CLASSICAL: Mozart, *Clarinet Concerto in A major, K622*
ROMANTIC: Chopin, *Nocturne in D♭, Op.27 No.2*
EARLY 20TH CENTURY: Copland, *Appalachian Spring*; Bartók, *Suite, Op.14*
CONTEMPORARY: Philip Glass, film score, *The Hours*

The aim of the test

The purpose of this test is to develop your aural perception. It encourages you to listen to music rather than just hearing it.

SURVIVAL TIPS — Test 8D

1. The examiner will not normally ask specific questions, but ask you to describe the piece.

2. Try to describe as many features as possible as these will often help you to decide on the style and period of the piece.

3. If you find it difficult to remember all the features you have heard, at least describe: **Character**; **Texture**; **Style and Period**.

4. Be prepared to answer supplementary questions. Don't be content with one-word answers.

5. When describing the character of a piece, don't be afraid of saying what immediately comes into your head. If it sounds jazzy and off-beat, say so but say SOMETHING – you may get something right. If you say nothing you will get nothing right.

6. If you cannot think of a way of describing texture, start by deciding whether it is "thick" or "thin". Then try to describe the separate parts.

7. If you can't decide when a piece was composed, start by deciding when it wasn't composed. If you're still uncertain, say something like "late romantic/early twentieth century."

8. If you find it difficult to describe a distinctive rhythm, clap it instead.

9. Use Italian terms wherever possible.

Put the music into words

FIND OUT THE MEANING

Accelerando, stringendo – gradually getting faster
Acciaccatura – crushed note (♪)
Adagio – slow
Agitato – agitated
Allegretto – moderately quick
Allegro – quick and lively
Allemande – baroque dance-form in moderate duple time
Anacrusis – upbeat at the beginning of a piece or phrase
Andante – at a walking pace
Andantino – a little faster than **Andante**
Arpeggiated – like an arpeggio, moving by leap
Appoggiatura – "leaning" note (♪)
Articulation – how the notes are played or sung (smoothly or detached)
Atonal – having no key
Binary form – AB structure; one section followed by a different second section
Cadence – resting point at the end of a phrase
Cantabile – singing
Chromatic – moving by semitone step
Con brio – with vigour
Contrapuntal, counterpoint – two or more melodic lines played simultaneously
Courante – triple-time movement in a dance suite
Crescendo, cresc. – gradually getting louder
Diminuendo, dim. – gradually getting quieter
Dissonance – discordant, clashing
Dolce – sweet
Dominant – the fifth note of the scale
Dynamics – how loudly or quietly the notes are played or sung
Energico – energetic
Forte, f – loud
Fortissimo, ff – very loud
Gavotte – baroque dance in 2-time
Gigue – lively dance-suite movement in compound time
Grazioso – graceful
Homophonic – chordal, all parts moving together